Dark Objects

Leya Noir

Dark Objects

ISBN: 9781707025473

DEDICATION

This is for anyone who has ever been moved by my words. For anyone whose words I've been moved by. This is for the ones who have stayed, and even for the ones who went away. This is for you.

CONTENTS

i   acknowledgments

3   unmanageable

37   every brand of fire

85   on awakening

129   index

I don't write like I used to,
and that's both sad and exciting.

ACKNOWLEDGMENTS

Thank you to everyone who has touched my life and given me inspiration for my words. Thank you to anyone who has ever bought a book for giving my words a home. Cover art by Ian Espinosa.

unmanageable

enthralled

I no longer have a past
for the masses are much more enthralled
by the mysterious girls
who came from nowhere
and built something
out of nothing
I no longer have a name
(no one could pronounce it anyway)
and I no longer have a face
(I use too much powder, concealer, and base)
and I'm perfectly fine
pretending that you were never mine

wanderlust

it feels dangerously familiar
-this fire-
it heats up my chest
and gets mistaken for desire
but it's really just wanderlust
and my addiction to getting higher

spin

I used to play spin the bottle
and desire to kiss the bottle
more than whoever it would land on
I couldn't recall the longest I'd ever gone
without a drink
but I remember spending two years
sober and obsessed with a windy city soul
only for the wind to blow them away from me

The overlap happened when
my lips found that sobriety wasn't
my cup of tea
and I got more love in the club than I ever did
from my bed

So I spread my wings
(along with other things)
and I spent two more years
naked and drunk with someone
who is probably still naked and drunk

and then I finally found you
but I realized I had a lot more suffering
to do
(and believe me, I fucking did it)

So now I just sit here
older and sober
reading The Love Song of J. Alfred Prufrock
wishing my life had been
measured out in coffee spoons
instead of sleepless nights
and whiskey neats

snooze

I pushed the snooze button
on my alarm
about five times this morning
I keep trying to push back
the memories of you
but eventually, I'll have to let you in:

reluctantly

I've gotten to know the cracks
in my ceiling
like the back of my hand
and guess what?
They look exactly the same
whether you're on top of me
or not

dust

and just like that
one day I won't be here
my bones will turn to dust
and that dust will blow away
in the wind
and the wind will whisper
the story of how the dust
was once bones of a girl
who had almost tasted love

drink

it's easier to hold
a drink
than hold
a conversation
and that's why
all I want to do
is quietly
hold you

god

I found god in a cold,
shitty room
and I found god
in this warm bed,
with you

and I found myself
in more ways than one

for the first time
in a long time,
it wasn't alone in my dark room
kissing the barrel of a gun

<u>surprised</u>

of all the things that I've survived,
I'm most surprised
by myself

roots

it's not to say
that my roots don't go deep

they do

it's only to say
that they can be transient

like a re-potted plant,
I'm yours

crushing waves

I'm trying not to fall in
too deep
or get swept up
by your crushing waves
I'm not sure if it's working,
but if that's not self-control,
then I don't know what is

anchors

I no longer look at people
and see only
anchors or life rafts…
some people are sailboats
meant to cruise around with you

…merrily, merrily, merrily

life line

now I'm living off
borrowed time
reminiscing about when the
substances borrowed all mine
counting down my palms,
the lines
every crevice that told me
I wouldn't survive

june

I promised myself
I'd never write
about the time
I took a life
(but now I'm going to break that promise
write it down and be real honest)
I walked away that day
with only scratches
(scrambled memories still come in patches)
you'll never walk this earth again
so now you live behind my pen

it's time for me to take my steps
and immortalize your last breath

dead

"you can't die from a broken heart"
they said
but hell, I tried
and I ended up dead
my heart still beats
and my blood is red
I just no longer see
anyone but you
in my head

<u>cracks</u>

you're going to go on
without me now
and I can't wait
to see what blooms
from the cracks
I left in you

<u>vile</u>

you loved me so much
and I held it against you
for what kind of vile creature
could love such a vile creature
as me?

slip

I feel it slipping
casually through my fingers
as if it were never there at all
but I know it will
always be there
to catch me when I fall

-the darkness

heretic

I always wanted to be tortured
so I chose the path
to self-inflict
desiring to non-conform
a self appointed heretic
and at the end of all these years
I finally found a place to stick
now all my tortured tendencies
are gone for my own benefit

<u>moon</u>

just like the moon
I'd turn my back
on your bad behavior
and just like her, too
I'd come back
thinking you could be my savior

ash

the last time I drove these streets
you were on your way to me

a smoky bar
a few Black and Tans

then we'd hide in plain sight
with my feet on the dash

watching time die
slowly with you
as the high fills your lungs
as we turn to ash

care less

I have been careless with myself
for I've woken up with arms
around me that I didn't recognize
and wouldn't want to
had I tried
I've been careless in the way
I've been under the influence
and in the way
I careen myself toward death

<u>moving day</u>

there's nothing left of us there

no trace

we patched up the holes
and painted the scuffs
so no one can even tell
that our love (or whatever that was)
had ever been confined
to those walls

rain checks

it's alright if it never happens
rain checks aren't real
and I can count the letdowns
on petals
asking if they do or if they don't
and when it all comes down
to the last one
waiting to be plucked
…well, I usually don't
even want to know the answer

wild

we were wild, weren't we?
I'd crawl and you'd scratch
and we'd scream like feral cats
we'd practice our dances
toward our deaths
and count down
our number of breaths
just to prove, by some grace,
we were still alive

-despite all the deadly things we tried

jameson

I gave you a bottle of Jameson
and told you to remember me
which is so contrary
to what Jameson
is used for
but you didn't need to drink to forget
it was all so inconsequential
that the memory would fade organically

it would dim quicker than the light
of the sun burning out
behind mountains

because the next day
you forgot all about me

little ghosts

I still remember the sound
of your last steps
out of my life
and the shallow indents
of your furniture
in the carpet
like little ghosts
reminding me
that what we had was real
and what we had
was over

daggers

I used to press flowers
into the pages
of notebooks
to cut the pain
of the words I printed in them

it was like trying to make
daggers look delicate

runaway

I used to be nothing more
than a lonely runaway,
but you've given me a place
to rest my head

bonnie and clyde

we used to need
to get high to pass
the time
and not think about
how we barely
made it out alive
but now that I'm no longer
the Bonnie to your Clyde
I've been stone cold sober
and bone dry

24/7

under lights
or under leaves
are the only places
that I can sit
comfortably
where my soul breathes

in this
"all or nothing" city
you're either dead
or really pretty
and even though
we have nothing to say
we scream for help
twenty four hours a day

sober

it was hard to tell
when I got sober
if the nightmare had just begun
or if it was finally over

<u>honey</u>

I'm a person who believes
that people can make mistakes
and come back from them

I went back to the honey colored liquid
(and your honey colored eyes)
the liquid was so bittersweet
(like your honey colored lies)
and if I could come back from you
(and the liquor)
anyone can come back from anything
ten times quicker

every brand
of fire

lovely

I recall when being called lovely
was something I strived for
and art was more
of a pleasure than a burden
but now here we are
with cards on the table
and marbles in baskets

and even though
nothing will ever be the same
I still sometimes desire
to be called lovely

mile high

you looked me in the eye
and asked if it was safe
but that's the illusion
when you're dealing with things
that break

-there's nothing quite as sharp
as another person's heart

nostalgia

you swore by the mantra
that the happiest memories
availed the most heartbreaking
nostalgia
which explains why
my heart has since
been breaking over you

<u>away</u>

they all go away,
anyway
(the things we love
all turn to dust)

art

I never thought
I was worthy of
the life I built for myself

first, I fixed my craving for drinks
(and other dangerous things)
I put a pretty young thing on my arm
and stopped causing self harm

and that's the delicate art
of mending a tattered heart

three's company

I keep wishing
you'd come closer
and the last thing
on my mind
is getting
sober
I just want to fill a cup
and drink it, and you, all up
this feeling is all I've ever wanted
you
me
and inebriation

...the threesome that always kept me haunted

<u>wind</u>

we spent years
drunk on our love
(and spirits, if we had a
few dollars laying around)
I can never forget what your lips tasted like:
the faint sting of loss and rye

every night would come fast
but morning would creep in
and I'd remember every sin

and now I remember feeling the wind
pushing you further away from me

progressive and fatal

they tell me
I have a flaw in my mind
(particularly the very deadly kind)

and that flaw tells me
that I don't have a flaw

…so now, where does that leave me?
in my 'all or nothing' mentality?

grey

I'm either all in
or I don't exist

I've never understood
the color grey

stamps

you left kisses
on my forehead
like stamps
trying to ship me off
to anywhere I'd be safe
not realizing how effortless
it would be
for a girl like me
to relocate

<u>sheep</u>

I've written down so many promises
to lovers that I couldn't keep

(the promises or the lovers)

those promises haunt me
so often that I still lose sleep

and now I'm left to my own devices,
counting broken promises
and long lost lovers
like sheep

jar

I keep memories of you,
of us,
in an airtight jar
labeled "do not open"
those little nightmares are
scary enough to destroy the world

hell

and then one day
we walked away
from each other
and from ourselves
and the only reason
I ever look back
is to make sure
your life is hell

magic

we were fucking magic, baby
can't you see?
it turned out better
than it was supposed to be
so when the devil comes
to look for me
please just hide me
in your arms

triumph

my biggest triumph
has been
in no longer
putting my heart
in other people's hands
asking them
to weigh my worth
and by becoming
a scale
of my own design

catharsis

it's only when I'm not
within arms reach
that you reach for me
I'm not the girl you used to know:
quiet and scheming,
getting high and dreaming
of you
of us
of guns and drug busts
of coming home with bloody clothes
where you've been,
I know I'll never know
eating breakfast with stacks on the table
under glocks and berettas
pretending we were stable
we lit fires to cook our food and your weed
and then we just threw it all away
because we knew it was nothing
we'd ever need

bloom

if flowers can bloom
from cracks in pavement
hearts can return
from desolation

loss

when you lose someone
you never had
why does it end up
hurting so fucking bad?

<u>brokenness</u>

there is so much more to us
than this brokenness

<u>pain</u>

I'll always be
in love with my pain

it's made me grow, so

everything/nothing

I have the universe inside of me
and I know
what it's like
to be everything
and nothing
all at once

past lives

have I ever told you
about how the pain
changed the shape of my heart?
probably not.
I try not to dig
too far deeply
into past lives
when I only lived
to survive

hurricane

some people are more hurricane
than human
and you should ALWAYS
heed their evacuation warnings

<u>former</u>

nothing really matters

the earth will spin
with or without you

I just prefer the former
to the latter

<u>russian doll</u>

I climb out of my skin
every time I let you in
becoming a new person
with each and every sin
…I am a Russian doll

wrong

I have mistakenly
held the wrong hands
while graciously
taken the lessons
they've handed me

<u>love</u>

love is an urban legend
passed down to keep
adventurous kids like me safe

a silly cautionary tale

yet, here I am
with all of this cursed blood inside of me
loving someone with every single drop of it

state lines

we cross state lines
and as the hours tick by
I find pieces of myself
in you

I can finally shed this skin
that I've never been comfortable in

<u>words</u>

I can't keep swallowing my words.
They're all I've got.

<u>ivy</u>

climbing
like ivy on an old wall

I've grown

you

-the sun
-you

the two most powerful forces of nature

beach

what would I do
if I hadn't found you?
I'd still be a lonely hurricane
with angry winds
and piercing rain
I'd bury myself when I met the sea
if I hadn't found you,
I wouldn't be me

metronome

you trace your finger
over my lips
like a metronome
and I feel a new rhythm
to my heart
that I've never felt before-
letting someone know
that you love them
could be the most vulnerable
and terrifying thing
next to dying
but I would be lying
if I ever said
I didn't love you

tarnish

it doesn't take
much dirt
to tarnish something beautiful

addictions

I've been losing things
that have been
important to me
like addictions and sleep
(things I always thought I'd
be able to keep)

it's in the lost little details
that I've come to find myself

ribbons

we have been broken for
so long
just like my
typewriter ribbons
and keys:

they no longer make the parts
to bring you back to me

<u>render</u>

have you ever felt your own heart
as an independent part
of your own body?
mine literally shakes
and renders me awake

I'm still in the aftershock of you

icarus

like Icarus and the sun
you are my one and only "one"

bump

tell me about those scary things
that go bump in the night
the things that would make me
reconsider my entire life
like how the human experience
isn't real
and how we're made by design
to be controlled
by the way that we feel
tell me about how it will be
the evil things that make us feel
most alive
like the ones with forked tongues
who are elusive by my side

linger

I'm always the one
whose love lingers
a little longer

but I don't mind it

the larger the cracks,
the more room there is to grow

your name

I used to say
your name
in the mirror
hoping you'd appear
but I guess my days
of believing in ghost stories
are over

<u>belong</u>

there will always be
a part of me
that doesn't belong
to anything

shelves

we hung our pictures perfectly
and stocked up all our shelves
of stories about our happiness
...and we believed that lie ourselves

ember

our embers burned
so bright that
I thought we'd end up
being third degree
but you just fizzled out
and ended up
leaving me with me

ribs

I loved you so much
that it damn near killed me
and now I sleep next to my own heart
because it doesn't quite fit
behind my ribcage anymore
and you sleep with anyone
hoping that if you close your eyes
tight enough,
I'll appear

last year

this time
last year
you were my ticket
out of here
but you turned out to be
just like the rest
devoid of the crucial thing
that beats in human's chests

on awakening

forward

if one of these days
I stop looking for you
what on earth will I have
to look forward to?

<u>sorry</u>

life gets a lot easier
when you learn to accept
an apology
that you're never going to hear

<u>bleed</u>

you can't put a tourniquet
around my heart
and expect the love to stop
bleeding out
it doesn't work that way

you need to let things breathe

<u>wolf</u>

you don't ever need
to throw me a bone, baby

wolves don't settle for scraps

<u>dreams</u>

my dreams and ideas
of you were more
magical
than you ever were
I broke my own heart
falling in love
with your potential

<u>bury</u>

when the day finally comes
when we no longer speak
please
just bury us in the trees

it will be you, me,
and everything we were supposed to be

movies

life is not like the movies
(but it was when I was with you)
and now that movie is over
the credits rolled, we're through
now you have your happily ever after
and I have my next script
but I have a case of writer's block
and I don't know what to write in it

(un)requited

stuck between
resolutions
and
regrets
wishing you didn't think I was
such a mess

there's nothing worse than unrequited love,
and nothing quite as common

with these lungs

with these lungs
I blow you out
like smoke
turn you into
beautiful shapes
just to watch you dissipate

hole

dry your tears
that hole in your chest
will be filled
one day

count

I used to count sheep
then I met you
and I started counting down sleeps
until we'd see each other again

and now I count on nothing,

not even you

<u>lucky</u>

oh,
the terrible things I've done
just so I could become
this lucky little devil
who can wake up
next to you

collateral

when I tried to control
everything around me
my life became hard to manage
they say that "hurt people hurt people"
and unfortunately
we became each other's
collateral damage

hollow

you still don't think I'm hollow
even when I tell you how much pain
I've swallowed
you just brush the dirt
out of my hair
and ignore the bruises

<u>spill</u>

I used to have so many words
inside of me that they'd spill right out
…and I still do…
I just don't have anymore for you

<u>desert heat</u>

it's 110 degrees
in the desert summer
and now your blood
is boiling alongside mine
and you call me your little queen of this hell
and even though we want to run away
from this home that's dry and desolate
here in the West
it takes leaving to know what you've left

books

I like the way books smell
when they're new
but I equally like them when
they've been read
a few times through

I think that's why I continue
to run back to you

borrow

I don't usually borrow words
but today, I think I'll borrow yours
and tell myself that I love me
(you're the only person I've been
hearing that from, lately)

months

either
I feel nothing at all
for months
or every single thing
all at once

idk

they ask me
"what's wrong?"
and I don't know how to answer
it's like
I don't know what to do with my heart

<u>whole</u>

everyone should get to experience
someone loving them
the way that I've been loved:
so wholly,
completely,
and then,
not at all
(it's the only way to grow)

lips

I'm just the girl
in the room
with more words
on her brain
than on her lips
that no one wants
to take pictures with

hourglass

we had an hourglass future
and I cherished each and every
sweet piece of sand
that dropped out of the top
that I got to spend
with you

dizzy

this world
always made me
dizzy
(and so did
the whiskey)

martha

those days were better back then
when our bellies were full
of cheap beer
and we had yet to have
our first kisses

you still had a pink tinge to your cheeks
because you were still alive
not buried so far down
in the ground
away from me

I wish you could see us now,
we'd make you proud

bottles

and then there was a defining moment
that I remember
I stopped wanting to be with you
and I just wanted to become you
evil, cunning, not giving a fuck
so now we can drink
until the sun comes up
until all of our bottles are empty
and our lips can spill
over each other
and onto other people's lips
and none of it even matters

fiend

you lie through your teeth
and every time you're not around
you're like a drink I need
-addicted would be an understatement-
you're like the air I breathe
it feels like a drug
and just when I'm about to wean myself off
and become clean
the anxiety creeps in
and I crave you like a fiend

may

we met in April
but you felt more like May to me
I couldn't stop thinking
about what you and I
May be

nightmares

my nightmares are still dreams
compared to what my life
used to be

smoke

she is smoke

something you can see
but not hold in your hand
something you don't want to interrupt

rather, just enjoy her beauty for that moment

(smoke can disappear in a moment)

scrub

I've never met an inspiration quite like you
and now, I'm not able to scrub you out
of my skin
and the reality is setting in:
I'm just not me without you

blankets

I'm so tired of the things
that come between you and me
blankets, and those
early morning hours

lonely

I'll tell stories
of love and pain
of loss and gain
until only
my lonely
ashes remain

recovery

I've always been obsessed
with the idea of recovery
(the idea that I could take
my shattered soul
and patch it up
to the point where
water can't drip through)

continuum

someone once told me
that I write with knives
but that wouldn't be the case
had I not been hanging on
to certain threads
within approximately
an inch or so of my life

and those threads never did me much good
besides tearing the fabric leading me
back to you
(a simple task I never thought I could)

and even though we're laid to rest in a place
I never thought we'd be,
I'm more than peaceful
so RIP to us
to you
to me

stuck

our words sometimes get stuck
in the corners of our lips,
or at traffic lights

-brief interruptions-

and I wonder what we'd all have to say
if our words had a safe place to stay

<u>without</u>

when did it start to fade?
that light in your eyes
you kept on me

and when did our priorities change?
choosing everyone else over each other

I keep forgetting what made me
want you so badly in the first place
when it's so easy to carry on
without
each other

horcrux

the idea of ripping yourself into shreds
sounds so painful
that many won't go through it
but the war on both sides
of my bloodline
has rendered me
desperate enough to do it

old

I never imagined growing old

but now I only imagine growing old with you

you make me feel safe
like our words
and the way you're always
calling me home
like a lighthouse
to a ship

wonder

do yourself a favor
and find someone who isn't lost
…you'll save yourself so much
wondering
and wandering

SHE

I've been wrong for most of my life
but for some reason, she just feels right

index

4	enthralled
5	wanderlust
6	spin
8	snooze
9	dust
10	drink
11	god
12	surprise
13	roots
14	crushing waves
15	anchors
16	life line
17	june
18	dead
19	cracks
20	vile
21	slip
22	heretic
23	moon
24	ash
25	care less
26	moving day
27	rain checks
28	wild

29	jameson
30	little ghosts
31	daggers
32	runaway
33	bonnie and clyde
34	24/7
35	sober
36	honey
38	lovely
39	mile high
40	nostalgia
41	away
42	art
43	three's company
44	wind
45	progressive and fatal
46	grey
47	stamps
48	sheep
49	jar
50	hell
51	magic
52	triumph
53	catharsis
54	bloom
55	loss
56	brokenness
57	pain
58	everything/nothing

59	past lives
60	hurricane
61	former
62	russian doll
63	wrong
64	love
65	state lines
66	words
67	ivy
68	you
69	beach
70	metronome
71	tarnish
72	addictions
73	ribbons
74	render
75	icarus
76	bump
77	linger
78	your name
79	belong
80	shelves
81	ember
82	ribs
83	last year
86	forward
87	sorry
88	bleed
89	wolf

90	dreams
91	bury
92	movies
93	(un)requited
94	with these lungs
95	hole
96	count
97	lucky
98	collateral
99	hollow
100	spill
101	desert heat
102	books
103	borrow
104	months
105	idk
106	whole
107	lips
108	hourglass
109	dizzy
110	martha
111	bottles
112	fiend
113	may
114	nightmares
115	smoke
116	scrub
117	blankets
118	lonely

119   recovery
120   continuum
121   stuck
122   horcrux
123   old
124   wonder
125   SHE

Printed in Great Britain
by Amazon

39106742R00081